The Science of Living Things

What is a Forest?

Bobbie Kalman & Kathryn Smithyman

Crabtree Publishing Company

www.crabtreebooks.com

The Science of Living Things Series
A Bobbie Kalman Book

Dedicated by Kathryn Smithyman
For two wonderful children, Devan and Brody Cruickshanks

Editor-in-Chief
Bobbie Kalman

Editorial director
Niki Walker

Writing team
Bobbie Kalman
Kathryn Smithyman

Editor
Amanda Bishop

Copy editors
Molly Aloian
Rebecca Sjonger

Art director
Robert MacGregor

Design
Margaret Amy Reiach
Kymberly McKee Murphy

Production coordinator
Heather Fitzpatrick

Photo researchers
Jaimie Nathan
Laura Hysert

Consultant
Patricia Loesche, Ph.D., Animal Behavior Program,
Department of Psychology, University of Washington

Photographs and reproductions
James Kamstra: page 26
Robert McCaw: pages 7, 8, 12-13, 15, 16, 20, 28 (bottom), 31
Tom Stack & Associates: Erwin and Peggy Bauer: page 25 (top);
    Sharon Gerig: page 10 (middle); Thomas Kitchin: front cover,
    pages 4 (top), 21; Joe McDonald: page 25 (bottom left);
    S. K. Patrick: page 27 (top); Greg Vaughn: page 1
Michael Turco: pages 22, 27 (bottom), 29
Other images by Corbis Images, Digital Stock, Digital Vision,
and World Art Inc.

Illustrations
Barbara Bedell: pages 4, 6, 8 (top, bottom left and center),
    10 (middle right), 12, 14 (top left, bottom), 16, 18 (top),
    19 (top), 20 (middle), 20-21, 21, 24 (left), 31
Antoinette "Cookie" Bortolon: page 30 (top)
Katherine Kantor: page 9
Margaret Amy Reiach: pages 7, 8 (bottom right), 14 (top right),
    18 (bottom), 19 (bottom), 22, 23, 24 (right), 26, 27, 30 (bottom)
Bonna Rouse: pages 20 (top), 28
Tiffany Wybouw: page 25

Special thanks to
Billy Ormerod

Crabtree Publishing Company

www.crabtreebooks.com   1-800-387-7650

PMB 16A	612 Welland Avenue	73 Lime Walk
350 Fifth Avenue	St. Catharines	Headington
Suite 3308	Ontario	Oxford
New York, NY	Canada	OX3 7AD
10118	L2M 5V6	United Kingdom

Cataloging-in-Publication Data
Kalman, Bobbie
  What is a forest?/Bobbie Kalman & Kathryn Smithyman.
    p. cm. -- (The science of living things series)
Includes index.
This book describes the various types of forests, elements that make
up a forest ecosystem, the wide range of plant and animal species
that live in different forests, and the importance of forests to the rest
of the Earth.
  ISBN 0-86505-992-6 (RLB) -- ISBN 0-86505-969-1 (pbk.)
  1. Forest ecology--Juvenile literature. [1. Forests. 2. Forest ecology.
3. Ecology.] I. Smithyman, Kathryn. II. Title. III. Science of living
things.
  QH541.5.F6 S57 2003
  577.3--dc21

                                                    LC 2002012124

Contents

What is a forest?

*Most conifers are **evergreen**, which means they keep their leaves year-round.*

*In some parts of the world, broadleaves are evergreen. In other areas, they shed their leaves for part of the year. Trees that shed their leaves are **deciduous**.*

A forest is a natural area where many trees grow. A forest is more than just a group of trees, however. It is made up of many other types of plants, including shrubs, flowering plants, and mosses. A forest also includes the animals that live in it. Thousands of different types of animals live in forests around the world.

The trees in a forest

There are thousands of **species**, or types, of trees. They can be divided into two major groups. **Conifers** grow woody cones, and they have leaves that look like needles or flat scales. Pine, spruce, and fir trees are types of conifers. **Broadleaved trees**, or **broadleaves**, have flat, wide leaves with veins. Maple, oak, and chestnut trees are examples of broadleaves. Some forests are made up of conifers, and some are made up of broadleaves. **Mixed forests** have both conifers and broadleaves.

Many levels of life

Various species of trees and other plants reach different heights as they **mature**, or grow older. As a result, forests are made up of many levels. Very tall trees form the **canopy**, or top level. They get a lot of sunlight. Below the canopy is the **understory**, which is made up of smaller trees, shrubs, and **saplings**, or young trees. At this level, a forest is darker, since the canopy blocks much of the light. The lowest level, or **forest floor**, is made up of ferns, mosses, and other small plants that grow low, near the ground.

Constant change

Life in a forest is not the same from month to month, day to day, or even from minute to minute—it is always changing! The plants that make up a forest and the animals that live there must **adapt**, or adjust, to these various changes in order to survive. Plants and animals get bigger and change as they mature. During some seasons, there is less food in a forest, so many animals must move from place to place in search of things to eat. A flood or fire also causes a forest to become very different.

canopy

understory

forest floor

*Trees and plants of different heights make up the levels of a forest. **Rainforests** also have an **emergent** level (see page 23).*

Forests are communities

The living things in a forest—trees, small plants, and animals—rely on one another for survival. Trees provide everything in the forest with shade and shelter from bad weather. Many animals feed on parts of trees and other plants. Some animals also help the plants by spreading their seeds.

Even the tiniest animals, called **decomposers**, help forests. They break down dead plants and animals into **nutrients** and minerals, which return to the soil. Plants then draw these nutrients and minerals from the soil and use them to grow.

herbivore

carnivore

scavenger

decomposers

Food chains

All living things need energy from food. Plants are the only living things that make their own food (see page 7). Animals get energy by eating plants or other animals. **Herbivores** eat plants, whereas **carnivores** eat meat. Some carnivores are **predators**, or hunters. Others are **scavengers**. They feed on dead animals they find. The links between plants, herbivores, and carnivores make up **food chains**.

Trees need animals, too

Animals help many types of trees **reproduce**, or make new trees. These trees need insects or animals to **pollinate** them before they can make seeds. Many seeds need animals to move them to places where they have room to grow into new trees. Broadleaves often produce sweet fruits around their seeds to attract animals. The animals eat the fruit, but their bodies cannot break down the seeds. Later, they pass the seeds in their droppings.

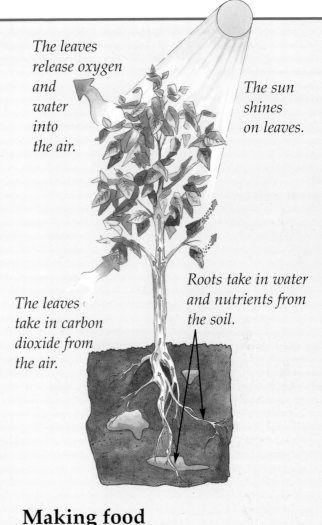

The leaves release oxygen and water into the air.

The sun shines on leaves.

The leaves take in carbon dioxide from the air.

Roots take in water and nutrients from the soil.

Forest birds, such as this scarlet tanager, spread seeds as they feed in the forest.

Making food

Plants use sunlight to make food. The process is called **photosynthesis**. The word "photosynthesis" comes from two words: "photo," which means "light," and "synthesis," which means "combination." A tree uses sunlight to combine water and carbon dioxide into food. It releases oxygen as a waste product. Trees take a lot of carbon dioxide from the air for photosynthesis, and they release huge amounts of oxygen.

How forests grow

As it rots, a **nursery stump** *provides young trees with nutrients and water.*

A forest is made up of trees that are at different stages of their **life cycles**. Even after trees die, they are still important to a healthy forest. When a dead tree falls to the ground, it soaks up water and slowly **rots**, or breaks down. It becomes a perfect place for mosses, ferns, and young trees to grow. Even if young trees do not grow on it, the dead tree breaks down into nutrients that become part of the soil. Other plants take in these nutrients, which help them grow. A tree that dies but remains standing is called a **snag**. Many insects, birds, and other animals nest and feed in snags.

The life cycle of a tree

Trees reproduce by making seeds. If a seed lands in a place where it can **germinate**, or begin to grow, it develops roots and a stem and becomes a **seedling**. In time, it forms branches and leaves and becomes a sapling. Over the years, it grows taller and its branches grow thicker and fuller. Eventually, the tree becomes mature and produces seeds of its own.

seed → seedling → sapling → mature tree

A forest forms

All forests form in the same way. Trees begin to grow in meadows and other grasslands. The first trees are called **pioneers**. They are tree species that need a lot of sunlight and room to grow. As the pioneers mature, their leaves and branches create shade and allow the seeds of shade-loving trees to take root. Over time, these trees also mature and reproduce. They eventually crowd out the pioneers, which no longer receive enough sunlight. As the new trees grow, the forest changes. When forests are left undisturbed for hundreds of years, they become **old-growth** forests. The stages of growth and change are called **ecological succession**.

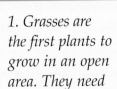

1. Grasses are the first plants to grow in an open area. They need a lot of sunlight.

2. Wind and animals carry seeds from other plants, such as flowers and shrubs, to the area. The seeds grow quickly because they receive a lot of sunlight.

3. In time, larger plants such as trees begin to grow. They compete with smaller plants by blocking sunlight and drawing large amounts of water and nutrients from the soil. Eventually, trees become the main plants. As they mature, the area becomes a forest.

Where in the world?

*The **taiga** is the largest single type of forest.*

There are many types of temperate forests.

Tropical forests grow near the equator.

Trees need a certain amount of warmth, sunlight, and rainfall to survive, so they cannot grow in the far North, Antarctica, or in deserts. Forests are found in almost all other areas, however. The **climate** and type of soil in an area determine which species of trees—and what type of forest—can grow there.

Climate

Sunlight, **precipitation**, wind, and temperature are all part of an area's climate. Different **latitudes** in the world have different climates. **Tropical** areas, which are near the equator, have hot, wet climates, whereas areas toward the North and South Poles have cold, dry climates. In between are **temperate** areas, which are cold for part of the year and warm for the rest.

Soil

Soil forms when water and wind grind rocks into bits. There are many types of soils. Some are more **fertile**, or have more nutrients, than others.

Forests of the world

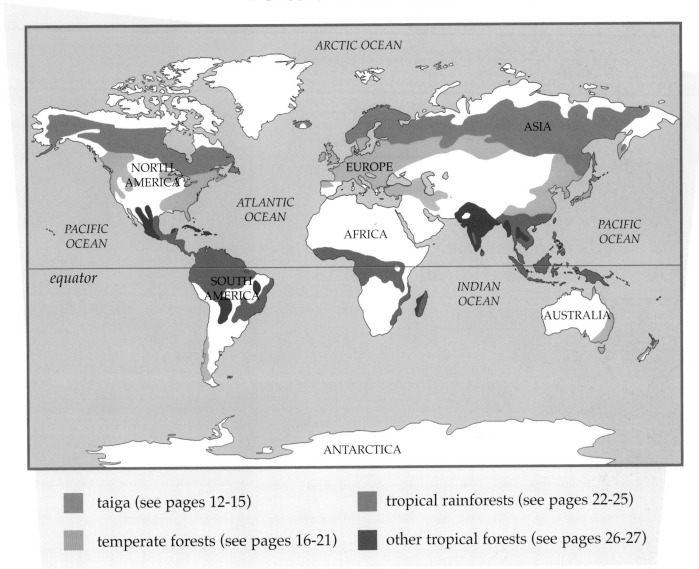

ARCTIC OCEAN

ASIA

NORTH
AMERICA

EUROPE

ATLANTIC
OCEAN

PACIFIC
OCEAN

AFRICA

PACIFIC
OCEAN

equator

SOUTH
AMERICA

INDIAN
OCEAN

AUSTRALIA

ANTARCTICA

taiga (see pages 12-15)

temperate forests (see pages 16-21)

tropical rainforests (see pages 22-25)

other tropical forests (see pages 26-27)

Biomes

Forests are **biomes**. Biomes are large, natural areas that have certain types of plants. Soil, climate, and the animals that live in these areas are also part of biomes. Plants and animals are adapted to the weather and other conditions. There are three main forest biomes—taiga, temperate forests, and tropical rain-forests. Within these major biomes, there are other types of forests as well. The map above shows where various types of forests are found.

The taiga

The name "taiga" means "little sticks." Taiga forests are also called **boreal forests**. They are found in the northern parts of North America, Europe, and Asia. These areas have short, warm summers and long, freezing winters. Most of the precipitation falls as snow rather than as rain, so boreal forests are fairly dry. They receive little sunlight for most of the year. As a result of these conditions, boreal forests have a short **growing season**.

Hardy trees

Only a few species of conifers are able to grow in the taiga—some sections of the forest have only one type of tree! Taiga conifers have adapted to the low temperatures, cold winds, and short growing season. Their short, needle-like leaves are covered with a waxy coating that stops them from drying out. Their branches slope downward, allowing snow to slide off without breaking them. The trees grow close together, which helps shelter them from the cold and wind.

*Trees in the taiga are so tightly packed that they block out the little bit of sunlight the forest receives. Few plants are able to grow in the taiga's understory. Mosses and **lichens** grow on the forest floor. At the edges of the taiga, the trees are more spread out, and other types of plants are able to grow.*

Fast forest facts:
Location: Alaska, Canada, Siberia, and Scandinavia
Temperature range: -47°F to 70°F (-54°C to 21°C)
Yearly precipitation: 16-40 inches (40-101 cm); mainly snow
Soil: thin, **acidic**, with few nutrients

 # Animals in the taiga

Animals found in boreal forests include moose, caribou, reindeer, lynx, black bears, wolves, weasels, hares, squirrels, owls, and chipmunks. Many animals, such as the elk shown above, move between the forests and open areas. Taiga animals have adapted in various ways to harsh weather and occasional shortages of food. Some move south to warmer areas during winter; some sleep through the coldest months; others are active year-round. Most taiga animals have thick coverings of fur or feathers to trap heat against their bodies, and many also have extra layers of fat to keep them warm. Some animals build up fat just for winter.

Plant-eaters

Large herbivores, such as caribou and moose, have adapted to the taiga's limited supply of leaves and tender plants in different ways. Moose usually stay on the edges of the taiga, where small plants and some broadleaves grow. Caribou are able to eat the tough conifer needles, and they also graze on lichens.

Heading south

Insects **breed**, or make babies, during spring and summer. Many insect-eating birds also live and breed in the taiga during this time. When the cool weather arrives, insects disappear, and birds **migrate**, or travel, south with their young.

Birds such as this downy woodpecker live in the taiga for part of the year and then migrate to warmer areas in autumn.

Hiding from winter

Many taiga animals survive winter by avoiding it. Several animals, including squirrels and bears, go into a deep sleep during the colder months. They do not actually **hibernate**, but they sleep for long stretches of time. Sleeping in their dens and burrows not only keeps the animals out of the cold, but it also helps them save energy because they are less active. They wake up on warmer days to stretch and look for food.

Temperate forests

Temperate areas have four distinct seasons: spring, summer, autumn, and winter. Trees and other plants grow during the warm weather, which lasts from four to six months. Temperate forests usually get rain in the spring, summer, and autumn. In most areas, snow falls in winter. Temperate forests are often called temperate deciduous forests because they are made up mainly of broadleaves that shed their leaves in winter (see pages 18-19). Most temperate forests have some conifers, however, and a few contain mainly conifers.

Fast forest facts:

Location: eastern North America, western and central Europe, South Korea, and Japan

Temperature range: -22°F to 86°F (-30°C to 30°C)

Yearly precipitation: 24-60 inches (60-152 cm); rain and snow

Soil: thick, dark, fertile

The leaves of deciduous trees change color as the days grow shorter and cooler in autumn.

Light in the forest

The tallest trees in temperate forests can reach from 60 to 100 feet (18-30 m) in height. Since the weather is less harsh than in the taiga, the trees do not grow as closely together. There is more space between the trees, so the canopy is not as dense. More light and heat from the sun reach the understory and forest floor than in a boreal forest. A variety of shrubs, ferns, mosses, flowering plants, and saplings thrive under the tall trees.

Saplings and shrubs grow between the mature trees.

In old-growth rainforests, trees have grown for thousands of years. Some have trunks that are more than 19 feet (6 m) across.

Temperate rainforests

Some temperate forests are located near an ocean, which helps keep winters mild and summers cool. These forests are also known as coastal forests or temperate rainforests. One such forest is located between the Pacific Ocean and the Rocky Mountains, where moisture from the ocean builds up against the mountains and falls as rain. This area receives more than 78 inches (198 cm) of rain each year! Many species of conifers, such as redwoods, Douglas firs, western red cedars, and western hemlocks, thrive there. The mild, moist weather is perfect for these trees.

Through the seasons

In most temperate forests, the broadleaved trees must shed their leaves in order to survive the cold winter temperatures. Their leaves are wide and thin in order to catch a lot of sunlight for photosynthesis. The leaves also release a lot of water. In autumn, when days grow shorter and cooler, there is less sunlight for the leaves to catch and the weather becomes drier. Eventually, the leaves die and drop off. Shedding their leaves helps broadleaves save energy. It also keeps them from releasing too much water and drying out. Without their leaves, broadleaves become **dormant**, or inactive, until spring. They live on stored food.

In summer, a mixed forest is lush and green, as both broadleaves and conifers have leaves.

In autumn, the leaves of broadleaves change color and drop off. Evergreen conifers remain green.

Leaf litter

The leaves that deciduous trees drop in autumn form a thick layer of **leaf litter** on the ground. Twigs, logs, and dead animals are also part of this litter. In spring, when the weather is warm and wet, the leaves and other parts of the litter break down quickly. They form a thick layer of dark **humus**, which has many of the nutrients new plants need to grow. As a result, the soil in temperate forests is very fertile.

Throughout winter, broadleaves are bare, whereas most conifers keep their needle-like leaves.

In spring, broadleaves grow new leaves. Plants grow and flower on the forest floor.

Life in temperate forests

Bald eagles feed on fish in rivers and streams. Many migrate south when the waters freeze.

Red foxes live all over North America in boreal and temperate forests.

Temperate forests provide food and shelter for a variety of wildlife, including bears, deer, porcupines, muskrats, foxes, skunks, squirrels, raccoons, frogs, snakes, worms, hawks, and bald eagles. These animals have adapted to living in seasonal forests. Some change their bodies to adjust to the seasons. Others change their behavior.

Wide ranging

Some of the animals that live in the taiga are also found in temperate forests. The northern edge of the temperate forest blends into the southern border of the taiga. Some animals move between the forests when seasons change, but others go from one to the other daily. Some birds and larger animals move between the forests to find food, and others travel in search of shelter.

Less food in winter

Many animals need to have different diets in winter than they do in other seasons. Deer and porcupines, for example, feed on tender young plants during spring and summer. In winter, however, snow covers these plants, and the animals must eat the bark off trees instead. Carnivores such as wolves often struggle to survive on less food during winter. Few small animals are active then, so hunting is limited.

Deer eat bark in winter. They can damage trees by stripping too much of their bark.

Snug on the floor

The temperate forest floor is a busy place! For most of the year, it gets enough warmth and sunlight for **cold-blooded** animals, such as frogs and snakes, to live among the plants and leaf litter. Many small animals, such as millipedes and worms, feed on the leaf litter and help break it down into humus. Other animals, such as birds and moles, feed on these tiny creatures. Even in winter, many small animals such as worms and insects are able to live in the litter. Although the weather is cold, snow on the ground acts as a blanket and shelters the leaf litter below.

Tropical rainforests

It is hot year-round in areas where tropical rainforests grow. The sun shines for the same number of hours every day, and it rains almost daily. The trees are broadleaves, but since the weather changes so little, most of them are evergreen. The growing season lasts all year, so trees can reach towering heights. The hot, wet climate is perfect for many other plants, too—these forests are home to more plant varieties than any other place on Earth.

Fast forest facts:

Location: Central and South America, western and central Africa, Southeast Asia

Temperature range: daytime 86°F (30°C); nighttime 68°F (20°C)

Yearly precipitation: more than 78 inches (200 cm); rain

Soil: thin, with few nutrients

Reach for the top

The trees of the canopy are so tall and dense that very little light gets past them. Other trees and plants have unique ways of reaching the sunlight, however. Emergents are trees that grow even taller than the canopy. Large woody vines, called **lianas**, climb up and over trees in order to reach sunlight. Some flowering plants grow on the trunks or branches of trees rather than on the ground, where it is too dark. These flowers are called **epiphytes**. Their roots dangle in the air to absorb moisture. Trees and plants that grow in the dim understory have gigantic leaves to catch as much sunlight as possible.

Poor soil

Leaves or fruits that fall to the ground break down very quickly in the hot, moist climate, and their nutrients are washed away by the rain. As a result, rainforests do not have a thick layer of humus. The trees are suited to the poor soil, however. Many have woody growths called **buttresses** at their bases, which give them extra support in the shallow soil.

emergents

liana

drip tip

buttress

Many rainforest leaves have long points at one end. Their "drip tips" allow rain to drain off the leaves.

23

Life in a rainforest

Tropical rainforests cover less ground than other forests do, but they are home to more animals—at least half of all the species in the world! More birds and insects are found in rainforests than anywhere else.

Finding a specialty

Millions of animals compete for food and space in rainforests. Most are **specialized**, which means they live in one level of the rainforest and eat one specific food such as a fruit or seed. The same food is available year-round, so animals do not have to change their diets, as they do in other forests.

Levels of life

Birds, bats, and small monkeys are found in the upper canopy, where there are plenty of fruits and flowers to eat. The lower canopy is home to larger, heavier animals such as larger monkeys, toucans, and sloths. Few animals live in the understory full-time, but many pass through or hide in it to escape from predators. Large animals such as jaguars, tapirs, and wild hogs are found on the forest floor. Millions of spiders, insects, lizards, frogs, and snakes live at all levels.

The Amazon rainforest

Brazil's Amazon River flows through the largest rainforest in the world. It is home to millions of different animals. Many of these animals are not found anywhere else. Most of the Amazon forest is so thick that it is difficult for people to move through it. Scientists believe that there are millions of animal species living there that have not yet been seen. Although people often think of monkeys or brightly colored birds when they think of rainforest animals, most of the animals are actually small **invertebrates**, or animals without backbones. They include insects, spiders, and centipedes.

Toucans may use their beaks to scare away enemies.

This katydid is just one of the millions of insect species that live in the world's tropical rainforests.

Many rainforest animals, such as the poison dart frog above, are brightly colored to warn predators that they are poisonous.

Other tropical forests

Not all tropical areas get as much rain as tropical rainforests do. Some areas are rainy for only part of the year. Other areas have unique climates and conditions that allow specific types of forests to grow.

In the clouds

Tropical cloud forests grow high on mountain slopes, where temperatures are cool and the trees are usually surrounded by clouds. Water droplets from the clouds collect on the leaves and branches of trees and then drip to the ground. As a result, the soil is very soggy and fertile. Cloud forests are made up of evergreen broadleaves, although other types of plants, such as ferns and orchids, also grow there.

Without this cloud forest to collect water droplets, most of the water in these clouds would not fall. Cloud forests add a lot of water to the surroundings.

Monsoon forests

Monsoons are storms with strong winds and heavy rains. In some tropical areas, a lot of rain falls during the monsoon season, but then little or no rain falls for the rest of the year. The trees in these areas are mainly broadleaves. In order to survive the dry season, they shed their leaves, just as temperate broadleaves shed theirs for the winter. The forests made up of these trees are called tropical deciduous forests, dry tropical forests, or monsoon forests. With less rain to wash away nutrients, monsoon forests have better soil than rainforests have. The soil is good for farming, so people have cleared many monsoon forests. You can read more about threats to forests on pages 28-29.

Orangutans in monsoon forests eat a lot of leaves and fruit in the summer to build up body fat. The fat helps them survive the dry season, when there is less food.

Mangrove forests

Mangrove trees grow along coastlines in tropical areas all over the world. They have **aerial** roots that allow them to live in water. These roots trap so much sand and mud that a group of mangroves can form an island, as shown left. Many shorebirds, shellfish, and mammals, such as monkeys, live on mangrove islands.

Forests in danger

When a fire does not burn out of control, it can actually help a forest by clearing away dead branches and trees.

People try to replace forests by planting new trees, but "tree farms" never have the variety of trees that can be found in a natural forest.

Areas of a forest can be destroyed by natural causes such as floods or fires that are sparked by lightning. This damage is simply part of the forest's life, however, and usually does not threaten its survival. The trees in damaged areas may die, but they return their nutrients to the soil and help new plants grow in the forest.

Wiping out forests

People damage forests much more than natural threats do, and the destruction we cause is usually permanent. People clear forests to make room for farms, ranches, roads, and buildings and to use the trees for wood and paper products. The pollution people create is also a big problem. Many trees are threatened by **acid rain**, which is caused when air pollution from cars and factories mixes with clouds and then falls as a part of rain or snow. Acid rain damages leaves and causes them to fall off. Without their leaves, trees can no longer make food and they die. Acid rain also poisons forest soils. Old trees are damaged, and new trees cannot grow.

Gone for good

In many areas of the world, including tropical rainforests, people **clear-cut** forests. When forests are clear-cut, every tree and plant is chopped down or burned, but only a few of the trees are actually used. Clear-cutting has serious consequences. The trees disappear, and so do the animals and other plants that make up the forest community. A species of plant or animal that lived only in that section of forest can become **extinct** very quickly—sometimes in a single day!

Managed forests

Some logging companies **reforest**, or plant new trees after they clear an area. Reforested areas are not the same as natural forests, however. Companies usually plant only a few species of trees. With fewer types of trees, these "tree farms" can never be home to the same number of animals and plants found in the original forest. Other companies are beginning to use **selective logging**. They cut down only the mature trees that they want and leave the rest.

The world needs forests

Forests are home to much of the world's unique and important wildlife. Plants and animals that can only survive in certain forests may become extinct if their homes are destroyed. By saving their **habitats**, we can also preserve a huge number of species.

Not just dirt

Soil is an important part of the environment. Healthy soil allows plants to grow. The plants in forests help prevent soil erosion. Tree roots grow in soil and help keep it in place. If soil is not anchored by plant roots, it can dry out and **erode**, or get carried away by wind or water. When trees are cleared, their roots no longer hold the soil and it gets washed away. Fewer plants can grow because there is less soil. With fewer plants rotting and returning nutrients to the soil, the soil's quality worsens. When a forest is cleared, the soil often erodes so much that nothing can grow there anymore.

Destroying forests affects animals that do not even live in them. For example, when eroded soil washes into streams, it destroys fish habitats.

Forests help it rain

Although some of the rain in a healthy forest is used by the plants, they **transpire**, or release any water they do not need. The moisture rises into the air and forms clouds, which eventually produce more rain. Rainforests add so much moisture to the air that the precipitation they create affects the entire world. Scientists believe that cutting down too much rainforest will cause **droughts**, or extremely dry periods without rain, in other parts of the world.

Getting warmer

Trees in forests take in carbon dioxide for photosynthesis. By absorbing carbon dioxide and releasing oxygen, trees help keep the air fresh. Carbon dioxide is a **greenhouse gas**—it traps heat near the Earth's surface. As forests disappear, temperatures may rise and climates may change. Scientists do not yet know how these changes will affect the Earth and everything living on it.

Learn more

Learn what you can do to make a difference and help protect the world's forests. Get started at www.forests.org. To find out more about rainforests, rainforest animals, and how you can help, check out the Rainforest Action Network at www.ran.org/kids_action.

Glossary

Note: Boldfaced words that are defined in the book may not appear in the glossary.

acidic Describing soil with high levels of natural acids which prevent the growth of many plants

adapt To change in order to become better suited to the environment

aerial Describing roots that are exposed to the air, rather than being underground

cold-blooded Describing an animal with a body temperature that changes with the temperature of the environment

deciduous Describing a tree that sheds its leaves during certain seasons

evergreen Describing a tree that keeps its leaves year-round

extinct Describing a plant or an animal that is no longer found on Earth

growing season The length of time each year when conditions are right for plants to grow

habitat The area or environment in which a certain plant or animal lives

hibernate An animal's winter sleep during which its heartbeat and breathing slow down and its body temperature drops to near freezing

latitude Distance north or south of the equator, measured in degrees

lichen A crustlike fungus that grows on rocks or tree trunks

nursery stump The base of an old dead tree that provides nutrients to young growing trees

nutrient A natural substance that helps animals and plants grow

old-growth forest A forest that has grown for a long time without being cut

photosynthesis The process by which plants use sunlight to combine carbon dioxide and water to create food

pollinate To spread pollen from the flower of one tree to the flower of another tree in order to create seeds and help trees reproduce

precipitation Any form of water, such as rain or snow, that falls to the Earth's surface

Index

1 2 3 4 5 6 7 8 9 0   Printed in the U.S.A.   2 1 0 9 8 7 6 5 4 3